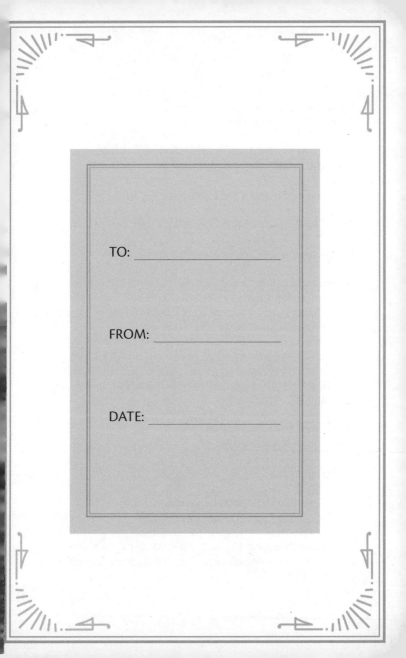

TO: _____

FROM: _____

DATE: _____

Published by Christian Art Publishers
PO Box 1599, Vereeniging, 1930, RSA

© 2022
First edition 2022

Designed by Christian Art Publishers

Cover designed by Christian Art Publishers

Images used under license from Shutterstock.com

Scripture quotations are taken from the Holy Bible, New Living
Translation, copyright © 1996, 2004, 2015 by Tyndale House
Foundation. Used by permission of Tyndale House Publishers,
Carol Stream, Illinois 60188. All rights reserved.

Scripture quotations are taken from the Holy Bible, New
International Version®, NIV® Copyright © 1973, 1978, 1984,
2011 by Biblica, Inc.® Used by permission. All rights reserved
worldwide.

Set in 11 on 15 pt Cronos Pro
by Christian Art Publishers

Printed in China

ISBN 978-1-77637-117-4 (Faux Leather)
ISBN 978-1-77637-118-1 (Hardcover)

22 23 24 25 26 27 28 29 30 31 – 10 9 8 7 6 5 4 3 2 1

101 PRAYERS

FOR

MEN

ROB & JOSH TEIGEN

CHRISTIAN ART
PUBLISHERS

DEDICATION

To my sons, Josh and Mason.
I pray you continue to discover the abundant
life found in Jesus and the power of prayer
that is yours in His name. Love you always.
~ ROB ~

To my son, Reid Elliott Teigen.
I pray that the Lord is your God, and that
you bring all things to the Father in prayer.
~ JOSH ~

INTRODUCTION

Jesus offers Himself as God's doorway into the life that is truly life. Confidence in Him leads us today, as in other times, to become His apprentices in eternal living. "Those who come through Me will be safe," He said. "They will go in and out and find all they need. I have come into their world that they may have life, and life to the fullest."

~ DALLAS WILLARD

As you make these prayers your own, may you discover more of God's love and power to change your life.

YOU ARE MY SHIELD

---

*You, L*ORD*,*
are a shield around me,
my glory, the One who lifts
my head high.
*I call out to the L*ORD*,*
and He answers me from
His holy mountain.

PSALM 3:3-4

WALK THE TALK

*Dear children, let us not love with words
or speech but with actions and in truth.*

1 JOHN 3:18

Lord,
In Your Word You say my faith and beliefs are proved by my actions (James 2:14). I want the work ethic I talk about to show in my integrity on the job. My affectionate words need to be matched by giving, serving, and protecting the ones I love.

My neighbors need a friend who shows up in their struggles instead of just a "nice guy" next door. Instead of just preaching the truth, I need it to influence the way I speak and act in every situation.

Help me to not just read the Bible but to do what it says. Show me how to walk in the Spirit and bear the real-world, practical fruits of kindness, faithfulness, and self-control. May my walk match my talk as I live for You wherever I go.

Amen.

LET THEM GO

Those who cling to worthless idols
turn away from God's love for them.

JONAH 2:8

Lord,

Every single day I'm enticed to turn from Your love. I crave physical pleasure. I look to others to boost my ego. I work for success to feel important and safe. Yet when I pursue those things, I reject Your great love that can satisfy like nothing else.

Protect me from substituting any relationship, experience, or goal for You in my life. Give me courage to lay down the idols that compete for my attention and devotion. I want to grow in love for You and the knowledge of Your love for me.

Help me to "throw off everything that hinders and the sin that so easily entangles" so I'm Yours and Yours alone (Hebrews 12:1). Keep me close so I hear Your voice and depend on You for all I need.

Amen.

MIGHTY TO SAVE

The LORD your God is with you,
the Mighty Warrior who saves.

ZEPHANIAH 3:17

Lord,

My loved one is drowning in problems with no rescue in sight. Every attempt to overcome has failed. In the confusion, despair is setting in. Without Your guiding voice and mighty strength, all will be lost.

I know You're here. Reveal Yourself as the Mighty Warrior who saves the ones You love. Take control of the details of this painful situation. Show Your faithfulness to hear our prayers, forgive our failings, and provide what we need. Use this struggle to light a fire of faith as You demonstrate Your love.

Help me to hold on to hope. Teach me how to encourage with my words and help with my actions. Move through my prayers and do a miracle so everyone can know what an awesome God You are.

Amen.

BRAVE LOVE

Love does not delight in evil but rejoices with the truth. It always protects, always trusts, always hopes, always perseveres.

1 CORINTHIANS 13:6-7

Lord,

This world holds a twisted view of love. It glorifies violence and exploits the weak. The world rejects Your Word and Your ways.

Yet I desire to be a man who isn't afraid to love like Jesus. Who risks my popularity to stand up to injustice and speak the truth. Who has the strength to love my enemies without giving up. I want to do the right thing no matter the cost.

Make me a man who bravely faces the evil around me. Give me courage to step in and help those who suffer. Fill me with Your sacrificial love that will lay down my life for my friends (John 15:13). I want to be humble, generous, and full of grace like Jesus.

Amen.

GROWING IN GODLINESS

For physical training is of some value, but godliness has value for all things, holding promise for both the present life and the life to come.

1 TIMOTHY 4:8

Lord,

I can strengthen my body by working out and eating healthy foods. I educate my mind by studying and gaining knowledge. To stay competitive and advance my career and hobbies, I practice my skills and take all the advice I can get. I want to persevere and grow in every part of the life You've given me.

Yet as worthwhile as these pursuits may be, they can't compare to growing closer to You. Give me endurance to pursue godliness every day.

Show me the rewards for cultivating a relationship with You above all else. Remind me that earthly ambitions will pass away, but living for You holds promise for this life and my eternal life to come.

Amen.

SALVATION COMES FROM THE LORD

*I will offer sacrifices to You
with songs of praise,
and I will fulfill all my vows.
For my salvation
comes from the LORD alone.*

JONAH 2:9

GOD'S GIFT OF GRACE

For it is by grace you have been saved, through faith – and this is not from yourselves, it is the gift of God – not by works, so that no one can boast.

EPHESIANS 2:8-9

Lord,

Before You saved me, I was dead in sin. I gratified selfish desires and followed my own path. Even though I was made for You, I lived for myself.

Yet I was rescued by Your mercy. When I put my trust in You, You forgave my sin and rebellion. You brought me back from the grave and gave new life in Jesus. Now that I am made new, I have purpose, meaning, and can experience kingdom living here and now.

I want to take action and fulfill Your wonderful plans until You take me to be with You forever. Never stop your transforming work until You finish what You started in my life (Philippians 1:6).

Amen.

THE BLESSED LIFE

Blessed is the one who does not walk in step with the wicked ... but whose delight is in the law of the LORD, and who meditates on His law day and night.

PSALM 1:1-2

Father God,

Every day I'm faced with hard choices. Often, I feel lost and confused and don't know which direction to take. Give me wisdom to seek out godly counsel in my life decisions.

Lead me to the right people who look to You, are guided by Your Spirit, and see Your Word as the ultimate authority. Help me to surround myself with others who will encourage me to follow You.

As I look to Your Word for guidance, may Your Spirit fill me with love for Your truth. Govern my steps, bear Your fruit in my life, and bless my way as I follow Jesus in everything.

Amen.

GUIDE MY STEPS

*In their hearts humans plan their course,
but the LORD establishes their steps.*

PROVERBS 16:9

Lord,
It feels good to set a goal and run hard toward the finish line. As I chart my own course, I want Your blessing on the plans I've made. I confess I get busy working and only come to You when I hit a roadblock. Instead of letting You take the lead and set the pace, I try to run my life on my own.

Instead, teach me to seek Your perfect will for my work and my relationships. Show me how to abide with You in the good times and bad. Give me insight to see how You use my struggles and my victories to accomplish Your plans for me.

Thank You for walking closely by my side and holding all the details of my life. Make me like Jesus as I follow You.

Amen.

NEVER ALONE

Even though I walk through the darkest valley,
I will fear no evil, for You are with me;
Your rod and Your staff, they comfort me.

PSALM 23:4

Lord,

In this hurt, I feel overlooked and alone. I can't see my way forward through the dark valley of my pain. The challenges I face are intimidating and much is at stake. I want to believe You will lead me through this, yet all I can see is disaster and I'm afraid of what is yet to come.

I need Your reassurance that You are with me in the darkness. Show me how You protect me from harm and guide my way.

Take my anxiety and give me Your peace. Ease the burden I carry by helping me to cast my cares on You. Lead me to a quiet place of rest as I put my trust in You.

Amen.

A WILLING SPIRIT

Do everything without grumbling or arguing,
so that you may become blameless and pure.

PHILIPPIANS 2:14-15

Lord,

Heavy traffic or long lines at the store can sour my mood in a moment. People's selfish or immature actions can drive my frustration through the roof. Instead of serving others, I'm tempted to ignore their needs and please myself. Your call to do everything with a willing spirit is an impossible task without Your help.

Show me how to move from grumbling to gratitude in my heart. Set me free from the habit of dwelling on negative thoughts.

Give me discernment to see when I'm resisting Your will or struggling to believe what You say. Grow my faith so I trust You in hard circumstances. Replace my complaining with words of prayer and praise. Let Your joy be my strength so I'm diligent to care for the people in my life.

Amen.

GREAT IS YOUR LOVE

My heart is steadfast, O God;
I will sing and make music with all my soul.
For great is Your love, higher than the heavens;
Your faithfulness reaches to the skies.
Be exalted, O God, above the heavens,
and let Your glory be over all the earth.

PSALM 108:1, 4-5

BY HIS SPIRIT

"Not by might nor by power, but by my Spirit," says the LORD Almighty.

ZECHARIAH 4:6

Lord,
I keep crashing into barriers in life that I can't overcome in my own strength. My job can feel like a dead end. Bills demand all my money. My relationships grow one step closer and then move two steps apart. Temptations drag me into the shame of secret sins. Without Your Spirit's power, I fall to pride, frustration, and burnout every time.

Today I need breakthrough. By Your Spirit, empower and compel me to do everything out of love for You and others. Teach me to depend on You when I don't have what it takes.

Strengthen me from the inside out with bold, courageous faith. Keep me in step with Your Spirit so I know Your ways and Your will for my life. With You, I have all I need.

Amen.

GOD'S COUNSEL

I will instruct you and teach you in the way you should go ... Do not be like the horse or the mule, which have no understanding but must be controlled by bit and bridle or they will not come to you.

PSALM 32:8-9

Father,

I confess that I'm often stubborn and must be forced to go Your way. I say I want to do Your will, but when You tell me to step out in faith I'm too afraid to obey. When You instruct me to wait on You, I try to take control and make things happen myself.

Build my faith to believe Your promise to lovingly lead and provide as I trust You. Remind my heart that You're eager to reveal Your will even more than I desire to see it.

I know Your plans are best. I praise and worship You for Your faithful love.

Amen.

MY DELIVERER

"Call on Me in the day of trouble;
I will deliver you, and you will honor Me."

PSALM 50:15

Lord,

As blessed as I am, this sinful and broken world brings its share of trouble to my days as well (Job 14:1). The trials of life are hitting hard and I need Your help. After trying to fix the mess on my own, I've realized it's simply too difficult. I'm trusting and waiting for Your deliverance to come.

Help me to keep believing You hear me when I call on You in prayer. Since You've been faithful in the past, give me faith for the future. Give me strength when I'm worn down. Build up my courage to keep facing the fight. Teach me to worship You while I wait. When Your deliverance comes, may I give You all the honor and praise You deserve.

Amen.

A HELPING HAND

If either of them falls down,
one can help the other up. But pity anyone
who falls and has no one to help them up.

ECCLESIASTES 4:10

Lord,

All my life, I've been pushed to be independent. Self-sufficient. Quick to act and slow to show emotion. I'm praised for helping others but shamed if I need help for myself. Yet as my loving Father, You created me to live in community. You crafted friendship, marriage, and Your church so I could walk through this world with support at my side.

Show me how to develop authentic relationships with others. When I'm tempted to tackle my challenges alone, give me courage to reach for help. Make me transparent so I share my struggles with those who can help me grow.

Teach me to be a loving friend like Christ. Move me from loneliness to closeness with those You've placed in my life.

Amen.

YOU CARE FOR ME

Cast all your anxiety on Him because He cares for you.

1 PETER 5:7

Father,

I feel overwhelmed by the worries of this life. In my anxiety, I wonder, *Will I ever succeed? Will my health and my money hold out? How will my broken relationship ever be repaired?* The enemy uses trials to devour me with fear and tempt me to doubt Your love.

Today, help me to take the worries that cloud my mind and cast them on You. Give me faith to trust You as my rock and refuge. Remind me that Your shoulders are strong and wide enough to carry any of my burdens or troubles (Matthew 11:28-29).

Step in with power to help me resist the enemy and hold my ground. Surround me with believers so we can walk through trouble side by side. Give me courage in knowing You'll never leave me alone.

Amen.

BLESS THE LORD

*Blessed be Your glorious name, and may it
be exalted above all blessing and praise.
You alone are the Lord. You made the heavens,
even the highest heavens, and all their starry host,
the earth and all that is on it, the seas and all
that is in them. You give life to everything,
and the multitudes of heaven worship You.*

NEHEMIAH 9:5-6

I'M IN YOUR HANDS

When they hurled their insults at Him, He did not
retaliate; when He suffered, He made no threats.
Instead, He entrusted Himself to Him who judges justly.

1 PETER 2:23

Lord,

I see my coworkers and peers getting ahead at my expense. Friends and family betray my trust and cause me pain. My hard work and integrity feel ignored and unrewarded.

When I suffer injustice, help me to have the mind of Christ. Despite His perfect innocence, He endured horrible abuse and death so I could be forgiven of my sin. When I deserved punishment, I was shown mercy. Like Jesus, I want to trust myself to You as the One who judges justly.

Today, protect me from harm at others' hands. Use any hardship I suffer to teach me to endure and love my enemies. Your ways are perfect and You know what I need.

Amen.

FOCUSED THOUGHTS

*Whatever is true, whatever is noble, whatever
is right, whatever is pure, whatever is lovely,
whatever is admirable – if anything is excellent
or praiseworthy – think about such things.*

PHILIPPIANS 4:8

Lord,

You say to fix my mind on things above instead of earthly things (Colossians 3:2). Yet the constant bombardment of information coming through my devices fills my mind with ideas and images that damage my spirit and bring me down.

I want to learn to focus my thoughts on whatever aligns with truth, reflects Your beauty, and honors You and others.

Give me courage to say "no" to watching or engaging with anything that is destructive to my mind and faith. Shift my focus to what will grow my inner character. Keep my eyes on You and the beauty and life You've created. Fill my thoughts with Your wisdom, goodness, and love.

Amen.

A HUMBLE HEART

"For those who exalt themselves will be humbled,
and those who humble themselves will be exalted."

MATTHEW 23:12

Lord,

Life with You is a paradox that challenges my natural thoughts and feelings. You say if I want to stand out, I have to step down. Yet I'm tempted every day to aim for first place so I get noticed for my accomplishments. Forgive me for each time I seek the praise of people over pleasing You. And forgive me for my pride that thinks more highly of myself than I should.

Set me free from the futility of chasing after my own glory. Through Your Spirit, teach me how to consider others as better than myself and set aside my own selfish ambitions (Philippians 2:3).

Crush any secret cravings for attention and acclaim. I want to make Your name great in all I do.

Amen.

PURE JOY

*"Do not grieve, for the joy of the L*ORD *is your strength."*

NEHEMIAH 8:10

Lord,

Happiness is just a feeling that comes and goes based on my circumstances. True joy, instead, is the internal peace and hope I receive from Your Spirit in every situation. This joy can stay with me even when I'm suffering in the darkest valleys of life. When I grow weary in my search for happiness, joy offers me strength and contentment right where I am.

Fill me with joy that only comes from Your presence (Psalm 16:11). Keep me from grieving my past sins and mistakes instead of celebrating Your mercy in my life. Make me strong when I suffer by building my faith in Your love.

Give me steady hope as I trust in Your promise to show new compassions every morning (Lamentations 3:22-23). With joy, I can face tomorrow.

Amen.

RUNNING AFTER RIGHTEOUSNESS

*For the love of money is a root of all kinds
of evil ... But you, man of God, flee from
all this, and pursue righteousness, godliness,
faith, love, endurance and gentleness.*

1 TIMOTHY 6:10-11

Lord,

I'm constantly tempted to find my worth in wealth and material things. I buy into the world's lie that I can chase comfort and pleasure without my devotion to You growing cold. Yet the truth is that my heart will love only what comes first in my life (Matthew 6:24).

Whether I have little or plenty, guard my heart from attaching itself to my money. Teach me how chasing after prosperity will keep me from growing in faith and love for You.

Refresh my insight into what's most important. Let me approach my finances with gratitude so I steward Your gifts well. Make me content so I desire heavenly treasure over earthly gain.

Amen.

SHOW ME THE WAY TO GO

---

*Let the morning bring me
word of Your unfailing love,
for I have put my trust in You.
Show me the way I should go,
for to You I lift up my soul.*

PSALM 143:8

LOVE THAT LASTS

*Give thanks to the L*ORD*, for He is good.*
His love endures forever.

PSALM 136:1

Lord,

Romance fades. Friendships drift apart. Loved ones are separated by distance or death. My journey of life leaves a trail of possessions and pursuits that failed to last. Nothing I grasp in this world is sure to remain. That is why Your love is so extraordinary. You give me the one thing that is unfailing, unwavering, and everlasting.

I praise You for loving me through all the ups and downs of my life. You've always been faithful. Your mercy has met me with each new morning and never comes to an end (Lamentations 3:22-23).

You amaze me with kindness and blessings beyond my imagination. Like a rock under my feet, You keep me steady no matter what comes my way. I have peace knowing nothing will separate me from Your love.

Amen.

THE FAMILY OF GOD

*[Jesus] replied, "My mother and brothers are those
who hear God's word and put it into practice."*

LUKE 8:21

Lord,

A religious family heritage won't earn me a place in Your kingdom. You don't call me Your son because I attend church or follow the rules. Instead, You adopted me into Your family when I put my faith in Jesus. Your love changed my life and I want to worship You in all I do and say.

Help me to know and understand Your Word. Provide godly teachers and mature believers to teach me Your ways. Show me how to put the Scriptures into practice as I work and care for my loved ones.

Give me confidence in Your promises so I follow You with courage. Let my faith be proved by how I obey whatever You ask me to do. Thank You for loving me as my perfect Father.

Amen.

HEAVENLY REWARDS

*"Be careful not to practice your righteousness
in front of others to be seen by them. If you do,
you will have no reward from your Father in heaven."*

MATTHEW 6:1

Father,

I need a humble spirit to fight my cravings for others' praise and recognition. I'm tempted to show off my work and accomplishments. My heart wants to feel accepted and even to appear superior to the people around me. Wrong motives can turn my good works and spiritual practices into a tool to boost my reputation.

As a follower of Christ, I am called to humble myself, do Your will, and bless others with a servant attitude. It is through humility that You will lift me up in the end (1 Peter 5:6).

By Your Spirit, make me a righteous man who lives to shine Your light in this world. Transform my attitude so I exist for Your glory and not my own.

Amen.

ALWAYS THANKFUL

Rejoice always, pray continually,
give thanks in all circumstances;
for this is God's will for you in Christ Jesus.

1 THESSALONIANS 5:16-18

Lord,

It's easy to give thanks when life goes smoothly and You answer my prayers as I hope You will. But lately, You've said "no" or "wait" to my requests and I struggle to feel thankful. It is difficult to hold on to gratitude and patience when You seem silent in my circumstances.

Renew my perspective to see prayer as an invitation to walk closely with You through each situation in life. Teach me to come to You with all my hopes and needs, with a grateful heart that trusts You completely.

Fill me with joy that endures in hard times. Help me to see Your goodness woven through whatever I face each day. May I live in Your will as I praise Your name.

Amen.

A TRUE DISCIPLE

*"By this everyone will know that you
are My disciples, if you love one another."*

JOHN 13:35

Lord,

It's easy to fill my days with spiritual activity. But without love, my efforts to study the Bible, pray, give, and serve don't mean anything at all (1 Corinthians 13:1-3). In this divided and hurting world, only genuine love builds a church that can offer hope and help to those who need You most.

When others are caught up in angry disputes, grant me grace to show Your love as a peacemaker. Keep me from a critical spirit that is quick to judge others who are different from me.

Give me a forgiving heart and humble spirit. Use my life and my church to break down walls and honor one another as equal heirs of Christ (Galatians 3:29). Let me be known as Your true disciple because I love like You.

Amen.

YOU GIVE WISDOM AND MIGHT

Blessed be the name of God forever and ever,
to whom belong wisdom and might.
He reveals deep and hidden things;
He knows what is in the darkness,
and the light dwells with Him.
To You I give thanks and praise,
for You have given me wisdom and might.

DANIEL 2:19-23

SHINE THE LIGHT

"No one lights a lamp and hides it in a clay jar or puts it under a bed. Instead, they put it on a stand, so that those who come in can see the light."

LUKE 8:16

Lord,

I see the injustice, sin, and brokenness in those around me and grow discouraged. I'm confused about how I can help or make a difference. Often, I wait for someone with greater resources or influence than mine to step up to do Your work or make an impact.

Forgive me for choosing to stay passive and letting busyness keep me from shining Your light to others. I neglect my neighbors who need the good news of Jesus. Give me courage to stop playing it safe.

Show me how to take Your power into the world to help those who suffer. Make me willing to serve and tell of You wherever I go.

Amen.

QUIET TRUST

In quietness and trust is your strength,
but you would have none of it.

ISAIAH 30:15

Lord,

Life is busy and the pressure to keep up the pace wears me down. I'm eager to wrap my hands around the best education, career, income, future that I can achieve. Too often I depend on my own strength to get me through. I deny Your offer to lead me down a better path to peace, rest, and a closer walk with You.

Today, help me to be still and truly know You are my God (Psalm 46:10). Give me faith to wait quietly for Your direction and the courage to do what You say.

Soothe my anxiety so that I listen for Your voice and trust in Your plan instead of my own. Show me how to rely on You for all I have and all I am.

Amen.

A WORTHY LIFE

As a prisoner for the Lord, then, I urge you to live
a life worthy of the calling you have received.

EPHESIANS 4:1

Lord,

True discipleship is not for the faint of heart. You challenge me to consider the cost before I commit to following Jesus. You call me to live in paradox: I must lose my life to find it, persecution brings blessing, and slavery to You is freedom from sin and death. If I try to hold on to my old ways, my faith and growth will suffer. I might fall away from You or miss out on the abundant life You offer.

Give me courage to pay the price to follow You. Strengthen me to step out in faith and obey whatever You ask me to do.

Keep me from making friends with the world so I am fully devoted to Jesus. In You, I have life.

Amen.

GOD'S REST

*"Come to me all you who are weary
and burdened, and I will give you rest."*

MATTHEW 11:28

Lord,

I'm past the point of physical exhaustion – I'm soul tired. I feel weary from striving and working to live up to who the culture says I should be. Even my time at church adds a layer of pressure to be a better Christian. A two-week vacation sounds wonderful, but I need something more. I need a deep inner rest that only comes from You.

Help me to place my fears and burdens in Your hands. Teach me how to rest so I experience true refreshment that connects me to You.

When I'm pushing myself too hard, lead me to quiet waters and restore my soul (Psalm 23). Take the load from my shoulders so I can walk in Your freedom and light. Fill me with peace and strength.

Amen.

NEVER GIVE UP

Blessed is the one who perseveres under trial because, having stood the test, that person will receive the crown of life that the Lord has promised to those who love Him.

JAMES 1:12

Lord,

You said that in this life I would have trouble (John 16:33). Today my problems feel overwhelming, with no relief in sight. I want to be a man of courage and endurance as I trust You to work in all my hardships for my good (Romans 8:28).

Give me strength and grow my faith in challenging circumstances. Provide wisdom and guidance to help me navigate these waters, no matter how long they last. Give me confidence that You are for me – not against me – when I feel alone.

Fill me with confidence by knowing no trial on this earth will compare to the glory I'll experience in heaven. Keep me going with Your love.

Amen.

CREATE IN ME A PURE HEART

Create in me a pure heart, O God,
and renew a steadfast spirit within me.
Do not cast me from Your presence
or take Your Holy Spirit from me.
Restore to me the joy of Your salvation
and grant me a willing spirit, to sustain me.

PSALM 51:10-12

THE SOURCE OF LOVE

Whoever does not love does not know God, because God is love.

1 JOHN 4:8

Lord,

Nobody loves me like You because You are love. You are slow to become angry, You're compassionate and full of grace, and You never treat me as my sins deserve (Psalm 103:8,10). You never leave my side, and You rescue and delight in me as Your son (Zephaniah 3:17). Because of You, I'm forgiven and set free to love others like Jesus.

Keep teaching me how "wide and long and high and deep is the love of Christ" (Ephesians 3:18). Show me what it means to love those around me in what I say, how I serve, and in the attitudes of my heart.

Keep me from holding bitter grudges or refusing to care for those who struggle. Let Your love show in me so everyone will know I'm a child of God.

Amen.

DRAWING NEAR

Come near to God and He will come near
to you. Wash your hands, you sinners,
and purify your hearts, you double-minded.

JAMES 4:8

Lord,

It is easy in this life to get wrapped up in my own cares, goals, and happiness. I fill my time with selfish interests and pursuits. I may give You what's left of me but certainly not the best of me. As my love for myself and my way grows deeper, my love for You grows cold.

Yet You say it's impossible for me to serve two masters since I will love one and hate the other (Matthew 6:24). You call me to choose You over everything else.

Today, help me to draw close to You to repent and be made new. Take authority over every area of my life. Restore the joy of my salvation so You take first place in my heart.

Amen.

GIVING OR GETTING

This is how God showed His love among us:
He sent His one and only Son into the world
that we might live through Him.

1 JOHN 4:9

Lord,

In my efforts to build a life in this world, I aim for a rewarding career. I pursue comfort and entertaining experiences. My heart is drawn to those who make me happy and boost my ego. I forget that life and love come not from getting but from giving.

You demonstrated true love by sending Your Son, Jesus. In the same way, He gave His own life to pay for my sins. I received Your love and kindness before I loved You in return.

Help me to receive Your good gifts by faith. Fill me with Your Spirit so I can love others without holding back. Teach me to abide in You so I never forget where my life is found.

Amen.

FAITH FOR LIFE

The righteous will flourish like a palm tree,
they will grow like a cedar of Lebanon.
They will still bear fruit in old age.

PSALM 92:12,14

Lord,

When I commit my way to You, the future holds no fear. You protect, provide, and give meaning to my life. You keep Your promise to complete the transforming work You've started in me. Whether I grow tired in my youth or aging years, You give strength and the assurance I'll have all I need (Psalm 37:25).

Thank You that in painful seasons that tempt me to quit, You help me to flourish. You invite me to stay close to You, my Living Water, so I can grow and thrive.

Teach me to "number my days" so I grow in wisdom and never take one day with You for granted (Psalm 90:12). Keep me faithful as Your son to trust You always.

Amen.

**35**

WASHING FEET

*After that, [Jesus] poured water into a basin
and began to wash His disciples' feet, drying them
with the towel that was wrapped around Him.*

JOHN 13:5

Lord,

Help me to have a better understanding of who I am as Your son. You created me in Your image and purchased me with Jesus' life. You have a plan and purpose for my life. Knowing these truths equips me to serve You and others no matter the cost.

By Your power, give me strength and courage to lovingly care for my family, friends, coworkers, and even my enemies as You lead.

Set me free from pride so I can live out my calling to serve like Jesus. Show me practical ways to lay my life down for others in tangible ways. Thank You for Jesus' humble heart to serve and give up everything out of love for us all.

Amen.

YOU LIGHT UP MY DARKNESS

O Lord, You are my lamp.
The Lord lights up my darkness.
In Your strength I can crush an army;
with my God I can scale any wall.

2 SAMUEL 22:29-30

SURROUNDED BY LOVE

For the LORD will go before you, the God of Israel will be your rear guard.

ISAIAH 52:12

Lord,

This life is uncertain. I don't know what the future holds for my job, my family, my health, or my bank account. The cares of this world distract me from following You with my whole heart.

Remind me today that I can face each day with confidence since You always go before me. My life is in Your hands. Help me to believe You are good. You never let Your children fall or beg for bread (Psalm 37:25). Comfort me with Your promise to go out in front to prepare good things for my future.

No sin or shame of the past and no mistakes or mess I make today will turn You away. I praise You for hope, patient forgiveness, and Your constant watch over my life.

Amen.

A STEADY HEART

*They will have no fear of bad news; their hearts are steadfast, trusting in the L*ORD.

PSALM 112:7

Lord,

In this world, I see disaster at every turn. There is no escape from news of destruction and pain. Life feels out of control, and I wonder where security can be found. I'm grateful for Your invitation to put all my fears and concerns in Your hands. I want to know You as "my loving God and my fortress, my stronghold and my deliverer, my shield, in whom I take refuge" (Psalm 144:2).

Show me how to see You in my circumstances so I walk in joy instead of fear. Replace my anxiety with godly fear of You, the One who is above all things.

Give me strength and assurance of Your promises so my heart can be steadfast all the time. You are my perfect peace.

Amen.

FORGIVEN AND FREE

The Lord is slow to anger, abounding
in love and forgiving sin and rebellion.

NUMBERS 14:18

Lord,

You know every time I lose my temper, give in to lust, or compromise my integrity. In my guilt and shame, I can hold back from drawing close to You. I distance myself and my love for You grows cold. I forget You are faithful to forgive and make me pure if I confess my sin to You (1 John 1:9).

Guard my heart from falling in love with sin and turning away from You. Give me courage to admit my wrongs and repent. Fill me with faith to believe You will create a clean heart in me, renewing my spirit so I can abide closely with You again (Psalm 51:10).

Your love and grace are greater than my failures. You give me all I need to follow You with all my heart.

Amen.

HERE FOR A REASON

"And who knows but that you have come to your royal position for such a time as this?"

ESTHER 4:14

Lord,

You say I'm part of a royal priesthood in the kingdom of God (1 Peter 2:9). You chose me and called me to live for You in "such a time as this." I want to be a courageous man who willingly speaks the truth in love to a world that is lost without You.

Give me confidence to step in to love, help, and rescue those caught in sin and despair. Protect me and provide wisdom so I'm safe from falling into sin as well (1 Corinthians 10:12).

Teach me to act with justice and show mercy wherever You lead each day. May I stand for integrity, truth, and Your goodness in my home and community. Keep me firm in faith until You accomplish Your perfect plans.

Amen.

BUILT ON THE ROCK

*"Therefore everyone who hears these words
of Mine and puts them into practice is like
a wise man who built his house on the rock."*

MATTHEW 7:24

Lord,

I'm tempted to trust in people who can't bring the peace I'm looking for. Politicians can't stop the world from going downhill. My hard work goes unrewarded by my company. Following the doctor's orders brings no improvement to my health. The most loving relationships don't cure my loneliness or insecurity. When I put my hopes in others' hands, I'm always disappointed.

I need Jesus more than anyone or anything. Teach me once more that gaining the world is no use if I've lost my soul (Mark 8:36).

Give me reassurance that heaven is my home and today's troubles will pass. Help me to build my life – my hopes and dreams, choices and beliefs – on You and Your Word alone.

Amen.

I ENTRUST MY LIFE TO YOU

Lord, show me the way I should go,
for to You I entrust my life.
Teach me to do Your will,
for You are my God;
may Your good Spirit
lead me on level ground.

PSALM 143:8, 10

READY TO LISTEN

The way of fools seems right to them,
but the wise listen to advice.

PROVERBS 12:15

Lord,

I'm afraid of looking foolish. I don't assume others will understand my problems or care when I struggle. I feel pressure to stand on my own two feet and tackle life on my own. Yet when I face job stress, broken relationships, financial issues, or temptation, You instruct me to seek counsel from godly people around me.

Raise up wise and mature examples for me to follow. Give me courage to bring my decisions and issues into the light by sharing them with those who can help. When I'm given advice, reveal Your will and wisdom in what they have to say.

Give me humility to listen, to receive honest input, and to submit to Your leading in my life. You are my faithful Shepherd who guides my course.

Amen.

CONTENT IN GOD

Keep your lives free from the love of money and be content with what you have, because God has said, "Never will I leave you; never will I forsake you."

HEBREWS 13:5

Lord,

This life is uncertain. My job, my health, or my bank balance could disappear without warning. I work and work to put more money in my pocket until I feel like a slave with no hope of escape. Yet You offer freedom and peace when I put my trust in You.

Guard my heart so I love You instead of money. Renew my perspective so I see all I have as a gift from Your hand. Show me how to hold my possessions loosely and use them to bless others.

Help me to want You more than any of the material things I crave in this world. You are my best reward.

Amen.

TRUSTING FOR TOMORROW

*Sow your seed in the morning, and at evening
let your hands not be idle, for you do not know
which will succeed, whether this or that,
or whether both will do equally well.*

ECCLESIASTES 11:6

Lord,

You call me to work hard and trust You for the future. Yet sometimes I hold back because I'm afraid of failure. Other times I refuse to wait for Your leading and I push ahead in my own strength. I need to trust that every detail of my life is held in Your perfect control.

Give me a willing heart to obey You in all things. Help me to love like Jesus, obey Your Word, and trust You with the outcome of all I do.

Give me faith to see You working in my life to take me where You want me to go. Make me Your good and faithful servant.

Amen.

WHO IS MY HELP?

Woe to those ... who trust in the multitude
of their chariots and in the great strength
of their horsemen, but do not look to the
Holy One of Israel or seek help from the LORD.

ISAIAH 31:1

Lord,

You offer yourself as my Source, yet I often choose to depend on myself or others instead. I trust in my income or budget to provide for my needs. I muscle through tough tasks instead of depending on Your strength. When my relationships struggle, I lean on self-help instead of Your perfect example of loving reconciliation. I go it alone and find myself stuck and stressed.

Show me how to lean on Your wisdom and invite You into the decisions I face in life (Proverbs 3:5).

Reveal Your best ways for me and give me courage to obey Your directions. Keep me faithful in prayer for all my questions and needs each day.

Amen.

ALL FOR GOD'S GLORY

*So whether you eat or drink or whatever
you do, do it all for the glory of God.*

1 CORINTHIANS 10:31

Father,

So many needs are grabbing for my attention. My job and family require time and energy, but I need room for friends, church, and personal goals as well. As I devote myself to all these people and tasks, I want to grow closer to You through it all.

As I go about my activities today, enter into every moment with me. Let me work and rest, care and serve with the help of Your Spirit to give You glory.

Give the wisdom and direction I need to set my priorities for the relationships and responsibilities that fill my schedule. Show me when to say "yes" and "no" to the opportunities that come my way. Teach me to worship You in all I do.

Amen.

I REPENT IN DUST AND ASHES

I know that You can do anything,
and no one can stop You.
I take back everything I said,
and I sit in dust and ashes
to show my repentance.

JOB 42:1, 6

TRUE FAITH

This is how we know we are in Him:
Whoever claims to live in Him must live as Jesus did.

1 JOHN 2:5-6

Lord,

It's easy to call myself a Christian or use the right words to sound like one, but I need Your Spirit to help me put my faith in action (James 2:20). I don't want to be a hypocrite who shows up at church, serves occasionally, and knows the facts but is unwilling to obey You fully from the heart.

When I struggle to do what You ask, remind me that obedience is how I show my love for You is true. Move me to live by the truth I believe.

Give me a desire to study Your Word and follow its teachings more and more each day. Above all, help me to obey Your greatest commandment to love others like Jesus (Matthew 22:36-40).

Amen.

ONLY YOU SATISFY

"My people have committed two sins:
They have forsaken Me, the spring of
living water, and have dug their own cisterns,
broken cisterns that cannot hold water."

JEREMIAH 2:13

Lord,

When I put my faith in Jesus, I was given new life. I no longer suffer guilt or separation from You. Your Spirit's power lets me experience life to its fullest as Your child. Instead of striving to earn a place in heaven, I'm secure forever. Yet when challenges come, I still look to others – and myself – for rescue. I stop depending on You as my Source and am left empty and wanting.

My help comes from You alone, and only You can satisfy my deepest needs. Refresh my faith and hope today. Help me to trust in Jesus instead of my own good works. Lead me to Your well of living water that never runs dry.

Amen.

PEOPLE-PLEASING

Fear of man will prove to be a snare,
but whoever trusts in the Lord is kept safe.

PROVERBS 29:25

Lord,

So often I worry about the approval of others instead of simply trusting You. This fear of people's opinions can make me resist Your will. I hold back when You ask me to move forward or rush ahead when You tell me to wait. I stay silent instead of speaking the truth in love, and my priorities fall out of order. I need You to set me free from this people-pleasing trap.

Forgive me for caring more about what others think than who You say I am. Give me the courage to obey You even if it looks foolish.

Fill me with confidence since "the Lord is my helper. What can mere mortals do to me?" (Hebrews 13:6). I want to please You more than anyone else.

Amen.

IN GOD'S HANDS

*But I trust in You, L*ORD*; I say, "You are my God."*
My times are in Your hands.

PSALM 31:14-15

Lord,

To gain a heart of wisdom, I must not take a single day for granted (Psalm 90:12). Never let me forget that my life is in Your hands, and each day is planned by You. No crisis is a surprise to You since You're fully in control. Help me to trust You when troubles feel overwhelming. Give me faith that my future is secure in You.

Through Jesus I am at peace with God and can live at peace with others as well. You save me from anxiety in the storms of life.

Grant me grace to trust You so deeply that I never fear what tomorrow may hold. I want my life to give You glory every day.

Amen.

TAKE UP THE CAUSE

Defend the weak and the fatherless; uphold the cause
of the poor and the oppressed. Rescue the weak and
the needy; deliver them from the hand of the wicked.

PSALM 82:3-4

Lord,

I'm tempted to look at this broken world and say, "God, do something!" Yet You say if I care for those who suffer, it's as if I'm caring for You (Matthew 25:37-40). You call me to stand for those who can't fight for themselves. I need You to open my eyes to see the abused and exploited, helpless and lonely in the world around me.

Give me courage to pray and take action to help others. Show me practical ways to stand in the gap for those in need.

Make me an authentic man of God who both listens to Your Word and does what it says as I serve in Your name (James 1:22).

Amen.

I LOVE YOU, LORD

I love You, LORD, my strength.
The LORD is my rock,
my fortress and my deliverer;
my God is my rock, in whom I take refuge,
my shield and the horn of my salvation,
my stronghold.

PSALM 18:1-2

READY TO HELP

God is our refuge and strength,
an ever-present help in trouble.

PSALM 46:1

Lord,

Life can feel dark, lonely, and painful at times. Yet when I'm overwhelmed by the size of my problems, You promise You are here. You listen to my cries for help and answer every prayer. As my Good Shepherd, You lead and guide me through the most difficult circumstances. Thank You for going with me through my toughest moments.

Keep me steady in faith even when I don't feel Your presence. If I struggle to see Your hand in my life, show me You're working in the silence. Keep me pointed in the right direction when I feel confused by fear.

Make me confident in Your promise to never leave me on my own (Hebrews 13:5). May I know Your comfort in my struggle as You fill me with peace.

Amen.

A WOMAN'S WORTH

A wife of noble character who can find?
She is worth far more than rubies.

PROVERBS 31:10

Lord,

Thank You for the amazing women who impact my life. You love and cherish wives and daughters, sisters and mothers as beautiful treasures created in Your image. Through Jesus, You show the worth of each of Your daughters. Yet this world has sexualized, abused, and devalued women. It grieves my heart and I want to make a difference.

Help me to give the girls and women in my life the honor they deserve. Teach me to value them as priceless gifts from Your hand.

Guard my heart from pride that refuses to esteem or elevate women at every opportunity. Let me serve my loved ones and sisters in Christ by Your Spirit. Use me to set an example of godly love and to respect the men who follow my lead.

Amen.

SLOW TO ANGER

Everyone should be quick to listen, slow to speak and slow to become angry, because human anger does not produce the righteousness that God desires.

JAMES 1:19-20

Father,

Forgive me for losing my temper too easily. I snap at my family, I'm impatient with friends, or I lose my temper with coworkers in moments of frustration.

Harsh words explode as people push my buttons or when I'm physically exhausted. When I don't feel heard, I overreact and take offense. Anger leads me to say hurtful words I regret.

Help me to be slow to speak and quick to listen to others. I want to be a man who seeks to understand before I react in anger. Guide me as I work to extend love and mercy to those around me.

May Your Spirit work so I can grow toward more kindness, gentleness, and self-control.

Amen.

DECLARE WHAT HE'S DONE

Declare His glory among the nations,
His marvelous deeds among all peoples.

PSALM 96:3

Lord,

When I'm excited, I like to share it with everyone. I brag about my favorite team's championship victory. I spread the word about a great new film or an exciting vacation destination. Prosperity and blessings are celebrated with the people in my life. Yet how often do I talk about Your amazing work in my life? Do I give You the glory You deserve?

Forgive me for staying quiet about all the good You do for me. Every answered prayer, forgiven sin, and blessing I experience is a gift from Your hand (James 1:17). Give me boldness to share how You're providing, helping, and caring in amazing ways.

Use my testimony of Your power to build others' faith in You. You deserve honor and praise from all people, all the time.

Amen.

WAITING AND TRUSTING

The Lord is not slow in keeping His promise ...
Instead He is patient with you, not wanting anyone
to perish, but everyone to come to repentance.

2 PETER 3:9

Lord,

With the evil all around me, I point fingers and judge others as I wait for You to right the wrongs in this fallen world. I grow tired of doing good as others get away with sin and grow more hostile toward You each day.

I need You to soften my self-righteous heart to remember Your patient kindness that leads to repentance (Romans 2:4). Every person on earth is made in Your image, and You desire each one to be saved.

You are slow to anger and abounding in love. Give me that same love for friends and family who struggle to know and follow You. Refresh my hope in Your perfect plan to make all things new.

Amen.

BE WITH ME, LORD

---

*Oh, that You would bless me
and enlarge my territory!
Let Your hand be with me,
and keep me from harm
so that I will be free from pain.*

1 CHRONICLES 4:10

STEPPING OUT

The Lord had said to Abram, "Go from your country, your people and your father's household to the land I will show you."

GENESIS 12:1

Lord,

It's intimidating to leave what's comfortable and familiar and follow You into an unknown future. I know what I'm facing is too big to handle on my own. It's unclear where I'm headed, but You're asking me to trust You despite my doubts and uncertainties. Stepping into Your will means giving up control of my life.

Give me the faith and courage I need to trust You wherever I go. Guide and light my path so I head in the right direction. Show me You're faithful and give me confidence in Your promise to reward those who seek You (Hebrews 11:6). Even if You walk me through dark valleys, be my Shepherd who gets me through. Keep me close to You forever.

Amen.

ANSWERED PRAYERS

You do not have because you do not ask God.
When you ask, you do not receive, because you
ask with wrong motives, that you may
spend what you get on your pleasures.

JAMES 4:2-3

Lord,

How amazing that You, the Creator and Lord of all things, invite me to bring all my needs and hopes to You in prayer (Ephesians 6:18). Like a kind father, You listen and care about everything I desire. Yet in Your wisdom, You also care about my heart and the real motives behind the requests I make.

Guard my heart from pride that wants You to solve my problems my way instead of Yours. Expose any greed or selfishness in my heart as I pray.

Teach me to use the gifts I receive from Your hand to love others and do what's right. Show me how to trust You in all things.

Amen.

GUARD MY HEART

*But a man who commits adultery has
no sense; whoever does so destroys himself.*

PROVERBS 6:32

Lord,

You warn me to guard my heart, because whatever I dwell on in secret will show up in my life (Matthew 5:28). If I allow lust to take hold of me, then adultery, addiction to pornography, or other sexual sin will be close behind. You set boundaries around sex for my good because You love me.

Teach me Your design for sex and intimacy and set me free to walk in Your ways. When temptation comes, remind me how sexual sin will bring pain and destruction to my life and those I care about. Provide godly accountability to help me resist temptation and do what's right.

Give me strength to run from any activity that empowers Satan to lead me to deeper-rooted sins. Heal any areas of my life where I'm broken.

Amen.

59

GOD'S GOOD GIFTS

"So I gave you a land on which you did not toil and cities you did not build; and you live in them and eat from vineyards and olive groves that you did not plant."

JOSHUA 24:13

Lord,

Every good gift in my life is from you (James 1:17). You've blessed me far beyond what I could earn or deserve. Yet this world sends the message that my own hard work can achieve whatever I want. That kind of self-sufficiency says I'm the master of my destiny and I hold control of my future.

Restore my gratitude for every talent, opportunity, and provision You've poured into my life. Guard my heart from worry over practical necessities since You know what I need before I ask (Matthew 6:8).

Let Your faithful generosity show everyone what a loving and powerful God You truly are. May I trust You always.

Amen.

YOU ARE ENOUGH

LORD, You alone are my portion and my cup; You make my lot secure. The boundary lines have fallen for me in pleasant places; surely I have a delightful inheritance.

PSALM 16:5-6

Lord,

Each time I try to boost my own sense of value and importance, the feeling never lasts. Yet when I pursue You, I am fully satisfied. Thank You that life is about more than climbing the ladder of success or building my status on this earth. You offer a heavenly inheritance based not on achievement but on my faith in Christ, who already accomplished everything on the cross.

With You as my portion, I have joy in this moment, hope for tomorrow, and a secure future with You.

When I feel insecure or inadequate, remind me that Your grace is completely sufficient for all I need and all I am (2 Corinthians 12:9). You are enough.

Amen.

THANK YOU, LORD

It is good to give thanks to the LORD,
to sing praises to the Most High.
It is good to proclaim
Your unfailing love in the morning,
Your faithfulness in the evening,
You thrill me, LORD,
with all You have done for me!
I sing for joy because of what You have done.

PSALM 92:1-2, 4

CONTENT AS I AM

*I know what it is to be in need, and I know what
it is to have plenty. I have learned the secret
of being content in any and every situation.*

PHILIPPIANS 4:12

Lord,

It's a daily struggle to feel content as I am. Everyone appears to have a better life than I do. I battle for peace with my job, my money and possessions, and my relationships. When I look for happiness in these things, I never have enough. Yet when I trust in You, I have peace through all the ups and downs that come my way.

Teach me to be grateful for all You give and even with what You take away (Job 1:21). Show me how to trust You to provide all I need.

May I always remember that when I walk with You, my Good Shepherd, I lack nothing (Psalm 23:1).

Amen.

TRUE RICHES

Why spend money on what is not bread, and your labor on what does not satisfy? Listen, listen to me, and eat what is good, and you will delight in the richest of fare.

ISAIAH 55:2

Lord,

I waste so much of my time, talent, and resources chasing after things that offer only momentary satisfaction. After a reward or a promotion, the joy is short-lived, so I strive for another achievement.

Entertainment and pleasure can only provide temporary relief from my stress. Nothing but Jesus – my Bread of Life and Living Water – can fill the void inside (John 6:35, 7:38).

I want to pursue eternal riches that will delight my soul. Free me from the trap of chasing the fleeting things of this world. Let me see each of my blessings as gifts from Your hand. May I praise You always as the Giver of all good things.

Amen.

PRAYING FOR AUTHORITY

I urge, then, first of all, that petitions, prayers, intercession and thanksgiving be made for all people.

1 TIMOTHY 2:1

Lord,

I can approach You with confidence when I pray because of Jesus. In His humanity, He understands my weaknesses and temptations (Hebrews 4:16). Since He lived a sinless life, He's completely qualified to stand in my place and intercede for me. What great hope this gives me when I pray!

Teach me how to speak with You (Luke 11:1-4). Give me courage to come to You boldly with my requests. Remind me that I can cast all my cares on You, whether big or small, because You love me.

Show me how to approach You with a trusting, thankful heart that believes You care and will answer in the best possible way. Fill me with strength to wait on You to answer in Your perfect way.

Amen.

A NEW LIFE

*Put to death, therefore, whatever belongs to
your earthly nature: sexual immorality, impurity,
lust, evil desires and greed, which is idolatry.*

COLOSSIANS 3:5

Lord,

Through Jesus, I'm a new creation. The old me who was helpless in the fight against sin can now choose to live by the Spirit's power. Yet in this life, I still battle temptations like lust, greed, anger, and bitterness toward others. I want to live as the new man You've made me to be, taking control of those thoughts and putting them under your authority (2 Corinthians 10:5).

Teach me how to walk in the Spirit so I don't gratify the desires of the flesh (Galatians 5:16).

Show me what sins I'm attached to that need to be put to death once and for all. Set me free by Your Spirit, so I stand firm and never let sin run my life again.

Amen.

GOD'S PURPOSE AND PLAN

But Joseph said to them, ... "You intended to harm me, but God intended it for good to accomplish what is now being done, the saving of many lives."

GENESIS 50:19-20

Lord,

I'm carrying pain caused by someone I thought I could trust. How do I move forward from this betrayal? Will these wounds ever heal? I want to believe You can accomplish good from this, but I struggle to find hope right now.

I know Jesus walked the road of hurt and rejection by those He loved – give me His heart to forgive. Help me to see Your purpose and plan, even if reconciliation never comes.

Strengthen me to place this situation in Your hands instead of trying to find justice on my own. Fill me with wisdom to know the steps to healing what's been broken. Let me know Your comfort, Your goodness, and Your power to save.

Amen.

PERFECT PEACE IN YOU

You will keep in perfect peace
all who trust in You,
all whose thoughts are fixed on You!
Trust in the LORD always,
for the LORD GOD is the eternal Rock.

ISAIAH 26:3-4

OUR GREAT GOD

For You are great and do marvelous deeds;
You alone are God.

PSALM 86:10

Lord,
Your greatness, perfection, and powerful works are in plain sight wherever I go (Romans 1:20). Yet I let the stress of busy days distract my attention, and I forget to thank You for all You've done in my life. You provide. Protect. Heal and help. You comfort my pain and teach me what's true. Everything good and beautiful comes from You.

Open my eyes to see Your mighty deeds and my mouth to tell everyone how awesome You are. When I'm tempted to chase the idols of my heart, show me that You alone are God.

Set my standard for love and justice so I show Your character in my own. Let all I say and do bring praise, honor, and glory to Your name. You are my everything.

Amen.

WHO IS LIKE OUR GOD?

Who among the gods is like You, LORD?
Who is like You – majestic in holiness,
awesome in glory, working wonders?

EXODUS 15:11

Father,

Today I thank You and praise You for who You are! No celebrity, world-class athlete, military force, or leader of nations is like You. You reveal Your power and love in my life all the time.

Forgive me when I sin against You by foolishly chasing after idols like money, success, and people's approval. I search for significance in gods that are not gods at all. When I fail to trust You, I feel empty. Everything falls apart. Yet You are always there for me, offering love and forgiveness every time.

You invite me into a close, personal relationship through Your Son. Prayers are answered beyond my hopes or expectations. Keep me devoted to You, my true God who never lets me go.

Amen.

WALK IN LOVE

Follow God's example, therefore, as dearly
loved children and walk in the way of love,
just as Christ loved us and gave Himself up for us.

EPHESIANS 5:1-2

Lord,

You are my example of love. When I was spiritually dead in my sin and far from You, You sent Your Son to save my soul. Jesus could have come and demanded I serve You, yet He served me by laying down His life. You could have sent Him as my judge, yet you sent Him full of Your mercy and love.

Teach me to love You with all my heart, soul, mind, and strength, and give me Your selfless love for those around me (Deuteronomy 6:5).

Get rid of any judgmental or critical attitudes in my heart (Romans 8:1). Keep me from hypocrisy that claims faith yet refuses to care for others. I want to be like You.

Amen.

THE GIFT OF WORK

*The LORD God took the man and put him in
the Garden of Eden to work it and take care of it.*

GENESIS 2:15

Lord,

You created me to enjoy hard work and to find satisfaction in caring for the people and things You've put in my life. Yet sin's corruption often makes work feel tiresome, stressful, and dull. I lose the proper perspective that I'm to work wholeheartedly for You in all I do (Colossians 3:23). My joy and motivation fade, and I grow self-focused and worn down.

I want to thank You for the reward of meaningful work. Give me strength to be diligent and faithful. Allow me to gain favor with my coworkers and those in authority.

Fill me with gratitude for my job since it's Your means of providing for my needs. Help me to trust You're at work in me each day.

Amen.

FORGIVING AND FORGIVEN

"And when you stand praying, if you hold anything
against anyone, forgive them, so that Your father
in heaven may forgive you your sins."

MARK 11:25

Lord,

I've been insulted and put down. Broken promises betrayed my trust. I've been wounded by those who should have cared the most. The price of forgiveness feels costly and even threatening to my well-being. Overcoming anger and resentment is a long, hard road. Yet You chose to forgive me. This forgiveness cost Jesus His very life.

Today, reveal any bitterness I'm holding toward anyone in my heart. Help me to forgive as You've forgiven me in Christ (Colossians 3:13).

Open my hands to release the person and the offense to You. In my own failure to love others, forgive my sin and teach me a better way. As far as it depends on me, let me be at peace with everyone (Romans 12:18).

Amen.

MY CONFIDENCE IS IN YOU

You have been my hope, Sovereign Lord,
my confidence since my youth.
I will ever praise You.
You are my strong refuge.
My mouth is filled with Your praise,
declaring Your splendor all day long.

PSALM 71:5-8

LIVING IN THE LIGHT

The night is nearly over; the day is almost here. So let us put aside the deeds of darkness and put on the armor of light.

ROMANS 13:12

Lord,

You are light, and in You there is no darkness at all (1 John 1:5). When my faith grows weak, I head for the shadows. I pursue my own pleasures and demand my own way. As I hide in the darkness, I say, "Not Your will but mine be done."

Shine Your light to expose any areas of darkness in my life. Move me to turn from sin and obey You in everything. Dress me in Your armor of light so I love Your Word and Your ways.

Protect me from the evil one whose lies will lead me away from You. Keep me always in Your presence because Your love is the light of my life.

Amen.

NEVER ENOUGH

What do people gain from all their labors at which they toil under the sun? All things are wearisome, more than one can say.

ECCLESIASTES 1:3,8

Lord,

The pressure to strive, chase, and go after more is wearing me down. My eyes land on bigger and better material things to pursue, and my ears hear of all the world says I'm missing. When I lay hands on what I've worked for, the satisfaction quickly fades and my heart craves something more. I need the peace and contentment only You can bring.

Become my source of true joy. Transform my point of view so I can see work as a blessing from You. When You give Your good and generous gifts, let me receive them with humble gratitude.

Let me trust You in my losses because I know You're in control and You know what I need. Your love is enough.

Amen.

ABIDE IN ME

"I am the vine; you are the branches. If you remain in Me and I in you, you will bear much fruit; apart from Me you can do nothing."

JOHN 15:5

Lord,

A branch disconnected from its vine is dead. You say if I stay close to You as my Source, You will answer my prayers and show me Your will. If I try to do anything apart from You, it will come to nothing.

Forgive me for the times I choose my own way and refuse to obey Your Word. Life is fruitless when I live for myself! Help me to remain in You so I can experience a life of purpose, meaning, and joy.

Show me how I'm depending on my efforts instead of Your goodness. Guide me back to You and take control of my life. May I remember that You hold all I need.

Amen.

74

DO I TRUST YOU?

But blessed is the one who trusts in
*the L*ORD*, whose confidence is in Him.*

JEREMIAH 17:7

Lord,

Sometimes it feels like my future success and happiness lie in the hands of other people. Other days, I'm tempted to believe my skills, tenacity, and personality can achieve my dreams and goals.

I care too much about pleasing others, and I base my decisions on what might boost my reputation. Putting my trust in others – or myself – is keeping me from receiving the blessings and help You want to pour into my life.

Show me how to put my confidence fully in You. Hold me back from pursuing fleshly satisfaction that brings spiritual starvation.

Remind me that though I may plan my course, only You can establish my steps (Proverbs 16:9). I want a humble heart that trusts Your perfect plans for every part of my life.

Amen.

SEX BY DESIGN

"'And the two will become one flesh.'
So they are no longer two, but one flesh."

MARK 10:8

Lord,
Sexual enjoyment is a gift from You. By Your design, You use physical intimacy to create beautiful oneness between a husband and his wife. Sex is so much more than a physical act – it's an expression of love that joins a couple together like nothing else.

Yet this world has distorted Your perfect plan for sexual intimacy. Men use pornography or betray their wives for their own pleasure. We're tempted to lust and experience sex outside the boundaries of marriage. I want to stay pure in heart and free from the trap of self-gratification.

Renew my mind so I hold a godly view of women and sex. Heal me from past sin and brokenness. Let me trust You and be a man who lives and loves like Christ.

Amen.

MY SALVATION IS IN YOU

Lord, I will praise You;
though You were angry with me,
Your anger is turned away, and You comfort me.
Behold, God is my salvation,
I will trust and not be afraid;
"For Yah, the Lord, is my strength and song;
He also has become my salvation."

ISAIAH 12:1-2

GOD'S GREAT NAME

He said to them, "When you pray, say: 'Father,
hallowed be Your name, Your kingdom come.'"

LUKE 11:2

Lord,

Your name is above every name ever spoken. Yet so many today are living far from You and want to do what is right in their own eyes. I want to be a man who honors You as great, mighty, and worthy of praise.

Just as I'm careful how I address my parents, my boss, or those in authority, I want to always treat Your name with respect and awe.

Give me courage to declare Your name in this world. Remind me that every time I speak of God, I'm proclaiming Your kingdom has come.

Fill me with boldness to tell of You and Your Word to everyone I know. Use me to reflect Your love and light so others may know how amazing You truly are.

Amen.

CALLED TO BE HOLY

*But just as He who called you
is holy, so be holy in all you do.*

1 PETER 1:15

Lord,

You chose me to be Your child before the world was even formed (Ephesians 1:4). Because of my life in Jesus and Your Spirit living in me, You've renewed my mind and my heart. I'm now able to say "no" to sin and "yes" to Your will for my life. I am set free to pursue passions and pleasures that align with Your holy ways.

Today, help me to walk in the Spirit instead of living to satisfy my old desires (Galatians 5:16).

Give me Your grace so my sole purpose is to please You in every way. Continue Your work of molding me into the image of Jesus (Philippians 1:6).

Bear Your fruit in my life so I am the faithful man of God You called me to be.

Amen.

HEAVENLY TREASURE

"Provide purses for yourselves that will not wear out, a treasure in heaven that will never fail, where no thief comes near and no moth destroys. For where your treasure is, there your heart will be also."

LUKE 12:33-34

Lord,

Your Word reminds me that life is like a mist – it's here one moment and gone the next. I cannot know what tomorrow will bring (James 4:14).

In the end, all the money and achievements I worked for will be left behind. My only lasting value will be in how I loved others and what I accomplished for Your kingdom in this world.

Thank You for the glorious inheritance You have in store for me in eternity. Teach me to use my time, money, and talents wisely since obedience now leads to rewards that last forever.

May the way I live and love reflect what's most important to You.

Amen.

PAYING THE PRICE

When we are cursed, we bless; when we are persecuted,
we endure it; when we are slandered, we answer kindly.

1 CORINTHIANS 4:12-13

Lord,

You sent Your son Jesus to be the perfect example of faith. By His suffering, He "learned obedience" to Your will no matter the cost (Hebrews 5:8). He left the glories of heaven to live as an ordinary man.

He trusted You to keep every promise as He suffered torture and death. Jesus made the way for me to believe, trust, and know You as my Father too.

Make me willing to pay the price of following Jesus. Set me free from any sin holding me back from pressing on toward You.

Fill me with joy – even in pain and persecution that might come my way – as I wait for Your rewards in heaven. Keep my eyes on You so I never give up.

Amen.

TRUST IN THE LORD

Trust in the LORD with all your heart and lean not on your own understanding; in all your ways submit to Him, and He will make your paths straight.

PROVERBS 3:5-6

Father,

It's tough to admit I can't do things on my own. You provide help through Your Word, Your Spirit, my loved ones, and Your church. Even so, I choose to rely on my own strength, abilities, and intuition to get the job done.

Help me trust and depend on You with the cares and worries before me today. Prompt me by Your Spirit to ask for help before I act, before I attempt to solve issues my own way.

Remind me that when I trust in You – even if it doesn't always make logical sense – You will direct my paths. You are faithful to meet my needs as I surrender to You.

Amen.

MAY I WALK IN YOUR TRUTH

Teach me Your way, O Lord,
that I may walk in Your truth;
unite my heart to fear Your name.
I give thanks to You, O Lord my God,
with my whole heart,
and I will glorify Your name forever.
For great is Your steadfast love toward me;
You have delivered my soul from the depths.

PSALM 86:11-13

THE BIBLE'S POWER

*I have hidden Your word in my heart
that I might not sin against You.*

PSALM 119:11

Lord,

The Bible is living and active and reveals what's truly going on inside of me. My heart is the hiding place of the darkest parts of my life – my sin, pain, fear, doubt, and shame – that I don't want You or anyone else to see. Yet when I let Your Word shine its light into those dark places, it offers hope and a pathway to freedom (Psalm 119:105).

Show me how to flood the shadows of my heart with Your Word. Teach me to meditate, study, and apply Your Word so it transforms how I live my life.

Use the Bible to renew my mind so I can recognize the enemy's lies and know Your truth. Guard my heart from evil so goodness and love flow from it to everyone (Proverbs 4:23).

Amen.

THE REWARDS OF FAITH

*And without faith it is impossible to
please God, because anyone who comes
to Him must believe that He exists and that
He rewards those who earnestly seek Him.*

HEBREWS 11:6

Lord,

Faith doesn't come easy. I'm just like Abraham when I refuse to wait for You and take matters into my own hands. Like Moses, I lose patience and react in anger to the ones You call me to love.

I'm like Your chosen people, the Israelites, who praised You one minute and complained the next. Yet even in their sins and mine, You call us men of faith.

When I stumble, put me back on my feet with perseverance since I don't run in vain (Hebrews 12:1-3). Keep my eyes set on You, with persistent hope in the eternity to come.

Give me grace to trust and believe, follow and obey by the faith I need today.

Amen.

LIGHT MY PATH

Your word is a lamp for my feet, a light on my path.

PSALM 119:105

Lord,

So many voices tell me how to run my life. Social media "experts," friends, and family weigh in on how to handle my plans and relationships. With all the input coming at me, it's difficult to discern what is wise counsel or just human opinion. I'm afraid I'll lose my way.

When confusion sets in, I need Your Spirit to direct me by the light of Your Word so I follow the right path. Give me biblical direction when I don't know which way to go.

Show me who I can trust for good, godly counsel. Grow my understanding of the Bible as Your Spirit helps me to study and apply what it says. Protect me from sin and destruction in my life as I trust and obey all You say.

Amen.

HOPE IN GRIEF

*Brothers and sisters, we do not want
you to be uninformed about those who
sleep in death, so that you do not grieve like
the rest of mankind, who have no hope.*

1 THESSALONIANS 4:13

Lord,

My heart is heavy with sorrow today. The weight of loss seems too much to bear. How can I face a future without the loved one who meant so much in my life? I'm holding on to Your promise to be my God who "is close to the brokenhearted and saves those who are crushed in spirit" (Psalm 34:18).

In my grief, give me patience to wait for healing. Let me hope in Jesus who overpowered death and will one day wipe my tears away (Isaiah 25:8).

Restore my joy in the morning after nights of weeping (Psalm 30:5). Show me how to comfort others with the comfort I receive from You.

Amen.

WAKING UP

"When he came to his senses, he said, 'How many of my father's hired servants have food to spare, and here I am starving to death!'"

LUKE 15:17

Lord,

I'm tempted to leave You to chase my own pursuits. Yet no kind of pleasure in this life can satisfy my soul's hunger. Unless I run home to You, I stay empty and starved for joy, peace, and the blessings only You can provide. You're my loving Father who calls me not just a servant but a son.

When I go my own way, lead me back home to You. Show me how abundant life in Jesus is better than anything the world can offer.

When I fear I've wandered too far to be found, remind me of Your kindness that leads to repentance (Romans 2:4). You're always ready to embrace and celebrate when I return to You.

Amen.

GUIDE MY STEPS BY YOUR WORD

The teaching of Your word gives light,
so even the simple can understand.
Come and show me Your mercy,
as You do for all who love Your name.
Guide my steps by Your word,
so I will not be overcome by evil.
Look upon me with love;
teach me Your decrees.

PSALM 119:130, 132-133, 135

DEAD OR ALIVE

*For you died, and your life is
now hidden with Christ in God.*

COLOSSIANS 3:3

Lord,

Some days feel more like survival than truly living. I become exhausted and discouraged, and I struggle to put one foot in front of the other. Yet You promise that through faith in Christ, my old life of futility is transformed into new life by His power.

Show me how to live the abundant life You offer through Jesus. Help me to resist the temptation to forget who I am and turn back to yesterday's behaviors and priorities. Release me from my "old self" with its selfish practices (Colossians 3:9).

Set my mind on eternal things that represent my identity as Your son. As I walk in the Spirit and live in You, fill me with new hopes and habits that look like Jesus. Grow my love for You like never before.

Amen.

YOUR FATHER KNOWS

*"Therefore I tell you, do not worry about
your life, what you will eat or drink;
or about your body, what you will wear."*

MATTHEW 6:25

Lord,

Anxiety fills my mind and steals my sleep as I wonder, *Will I have enough?* To ease this fear, I put in long hours at my job. I strive and save to grow my bank account. My full pantry, closet, and garage testify to my worried gathering and storing up for an uncertain tomorrow.

Reassure my heart that You provide all I need. Teach me to be content with what You've given. In times of plenty or struggle, help me to trust You with a thankful heart. Show me when I'm working in fear instead of diligence.

When the enemy tempts me with cravings for material things, keep me satisfied in You. May I pursue treasure in heaven that will never pass away.

Amen.

MY BATTLE

For our struggle is not against flesh and blood.

EPHESIANS 6:12

Lord,

In my daily struggles with stress, to-do lists, and relationships, I try to fix my issues on my own. I forget that my battles are not with difficult people or tough circumstances, but with "the spiritual forces of evil in the heavenly realms" that hate Your children (Ephesians 6:12). The world, my sin, and the devil work against my desire to love and obey Your Word.

When I find myself on the battlefields of life, teach me to go to my knees in prayer. When spiritual war is raging, give me courage to stand firm and resist the devil (James 4:7). Help me to overcome temptation and do what's right and loving.

Make me strong in Your mighty power so I can follow You faithfully all the days of my life.

Amen.

A MAN OF PEACE

"Blessed are the peacemakers,
for they will be called children of God."

MATTHEW 5:9

Lord,

This world needs Your justice and mercy. So many people are marginalized, exploited, and abused. The innocent are slandered or denied the good they deserve. A person's worth is decided by race or economic status instead of his or her true value as Your creation. You call me to "act justly and to love mercy" for those who need You most (Micah 6:8).

When the cost to work for justice seems too high, remind me what it cost Jesus to reconcile me to You (2 Corinthians 5:18). Give me wisdom to find peaceful solutions when it seems a fight is the only answer.

Make me quick to forgive and slow to get angry or lay blame on others. Help me to point others to Jesus as the One who can bring complete peace with God and one another.

Amen.

RELIEVE MY DISTRESS

*Answer me when I call to You, my righteous
God. Give me relief from my distress;
have mercy on me and hear my prayer.*

PSALM 4:1

Father,

Thank You for inviting me to be real with my emotions as I struggle through the difficulties of life. I don't want to pull any punches with how I feel. Give me courage to be open and honest with You.

Sometimes it feels like You don't hear me when I pray. Yet in my mind, I know this isn't true. Your Word tells me You hear and answer whenever I call to You (Jeremiah 33:3). In today's situation, make Your presence known in tangible ways.

Give me eyes of faith to see how You're working even as I wait. Calm my spirit so that I let go of worry. May I trust Your deliverance will come at the perfect time.

Amen.

KEEP ME AS
THE APPLE OF YOUR EYE

I call on You, my God, for You will answer me;
turn Your ear to me and hear my prayer.
Show me the wonders of Your great love,
You who save by Your right hand
those who take refuge in You from their foes.
Keep me as the apple of Your eye;
hide me in the shadow of Your wings.

PSALM 17:6-8

THE WORK OF YOUR HAND

Yet You, Lᴏʀᴅ, are our Father. We are the clay,
You are the potter; we are all the work of Your hand.

ISAIAH 64:8

Lord,

I like to be in control of my own life. I want to be able to call the shots in the decisions I make. Yet if I'm honest, I also want a powerful Creator when I'm in trouble or need rescue from my mistakes.

Without Your help, I can't overcome my selfishness or love my enemies. Only You can work the sin out of me by molding and shaping me to be like Christ.

Renew my faith that You use hardship in my life to work out my salvation. You are developing perseverance, character, and hope in my heart (Romans 5:3-4).

Through Your careful, loving, and patient work in my life, You are transforming me into the person You created me to be.

Amen.

A GIVING HEART

And do not forget to do good and to share with others, for with such sacrifices God is pleased.

HEBREWS 13:16

Lord,

As I'm caught up in life's busyness and caring for myself, I grow oblivious to the needs of those around me. You provide for me generously as Your son, so You call me to take what You've given and share with others. I need to slow down, look around, and see how I can share my time, talents, and resources with those who struggle.

Teach me to be generous and give with the cheerful, willing attitude You love (2 Corinthians 9:7). Show me who needs a warm meal, a place to stay, or a helping hand today.

Open my wallet to share my money and my schedule to offer friendship and a listening ear. I want to please You by trusting You to provide and giving with joy.

Amen.

BRAVE STRENGTH

"Be strong and courageous. Do not be afraid;
do not be discouraged, for the LORD your
God will be with you wherever you go."

JOSHUA 1:9

Lord,

I'm walking on unfamiliar ground right now. The giants I see on the horizon put fear in my soul. The uncertainties of life – my career path, financial security, health, and relationships – feel too difficult to overcome. I'm discouraged and wonder how to carry on.

Yet through it all, You say, "Do not be afraid." Nothing is impossible for You. In this moment, show me I have nothing to fear if You are on my side (Psalm 118:6). You promise to use all things for my good in the end (Romans 8:28). When all hope seems lost, nothing can separate me from Your love (Romans 8:38).

In You I have strength and courage to face the day. I'm secure as Your son for all time.

Amen.

MY NEW LIFE

I have been crucified with Christ and I no longer live, but Christ lives in me. The life I now live in the body, I live by faith in the Son of God, who loved me and gave Himself for me.

GALATIANS 2:20

Lord,

When I put my faith in Jesus, You made me new (2 Corinthians 5:17). My old self with its cravings and sin was crucified with Jesus on the cross.

By Your power I can say "yes" to Your will for my life. My hopes and priorities are shaped by faith in the One who loves me forever.

When I'm tempted to slide into old habits and attitudes, remind me who I am. Show me how to keep in step with Your Spirit. Continue to renew my mind so I live and love like Jesus. Keep me strong in faith until I see Your face.

Amen.

THE ONE I WORSHIP

"All this I will give You," [the devil] said,
"if You will bow down and worship me."

MATTHEW 4:9

Lord,
You created me to worship You, my Savior and God. Yet my heart is tempted to create idols that I put ahead of You in my life. I crave the generous gifts You provide more than You, the Giver of them all. My reputation and career, people and possessions become the focus of my love and attention.

Transform my heart so it loves You more than anything or anyone. Give me courage to resist the enemy who tempts me with lesser things. Keep me faithful in my allegiance to You so he has no power over my life.

Set my mind on things above that last forever instead of earthly things that pass away (Colossians 3:2). Nothing in this life can satisfy my heart like You.

Amen.

LORD, I CLING TO YOU

I lie awake thinking of You,
meditating on You through the night.
Because You are my helper,
I sing for joy in the shadow of Your wings.
I cling to You;
Your strong right hand holds me securely.

PSALM 63:6-8

CARE AND CONCERN

The LORD said, "I have indeed seen the misery of My people in Egypt. I have heard them crying out because of their slave drivers, and I am concerned about their suffering."

EXODUS 3:7

Lord,

I take comfort knowing You're aware of my circumstances and are concerned with my well-being. You understand the intimate details of my life and my emotions in every situation.

Today, I give You my fears, cares, and disappointments because You care for me (1 Peter 5:7).

I trust You're crafting my joys and struggles because You know what's best for Your children. As my Deliverer, You will rescue me from my enemies. I want to believe Your promises to protect and provide since "no matter how many promises God has made, they are 'Yes' in Christ" (2 Corinthians 1:20).

Turn my grief and fear to joy and hope because You never leave my side.

Amen.

TREASURES IN HEAVEN

"Do not store up for yourselves treasures on earth ...
But store up for yourselves treasures in heaven,
where moths and vermin do not destroy,
and where thieves do not break in and steal."

MATTHEW 6:19-20

Lord,

I'm tempted to put all my time and effort into establishing security on earth. I strive to get ahead in my career so I can build my bank account. Financial plans consume my thoughts. The distractions of this world draw me away from You.

Instead, give me a desire to invest in my eternal future. Help me to remember that everything I have is a gift from You, so I can be content.

Give wisdom to find the balance between active stewardship of all You've given and quiet trust in You to provide all I need. Remind me that everything I surrender to You now will be rewarded greatly when I see Your face.

Amen.

RUNNING THE RACE

And let us run with perseverance the race
marked out for us, fixing our eyes on Jesus,
the pioneer and perfecter of faith.

HEBREWS 12:1-2

Lord,

You challenge me to run the race of faith until the end. Yet the lure of sin, Satan's lies, and the trials of life can tempt me to quit. Jesus set the perfect example of a man who ran His race of trust and obedience, and He received the reward You promised. I want to fix my eyes on You so I, too, can finish my race in victory.

Help me to "throw off everything that hinders and the sin that so easily entangles" so I never give up (Hebrews 12:1). Give me endurance in the circumstances You're using to mature my faith.

May I be like Christ who "learned obedience from what He suffered" so I follow You with my whole heart (Hebrews 5:8).

Amen.

THE SOURCE OF POWER

*But He said to me, "My grace is sufficient for you,
for My power is made perfect in weakness."
Therefore I will boast all the more gladly about my
weaknesses, so that Christ's power may rest on me.*

2 CORINTHIANS 12:9

Lord,

Your wisdom turns the world's ideals upside-down. All around me, weakness is shamed and insulted. I'm pushed to accomplish success in my own strength, no matter the cost. Yet You say the secret to true power is to embrace my weakness and trust in You.

When I feel too small to tackle what's ahead, remind me that my toughest moments are when You do Your best work. Show me what it means to look to You as my source of help (Psalm 121:2).

Teach me to rest in Your grace instead of burning myself out. You will strengthen my soul when You're all I have.

Amen.

SAFE FROM THE SNARE

"Do not let them live in your land or they will cause you to sin against Me, because the worship of their gods will certainly be a snare to you."

EXODUS 23:33

Lord,

Every time I pick up my phone, I find temptation at my fingertips. Celebrities entice me to envy their lifestyle. Politicians offer their own wisdom to solve my problems. In this culture, it seems impossible to keep "not even a hint of sexual immorality, or of any kind of impurity, or of greed" from polluting my thoughts and choices (Ephesians 5:3). I lose confidence in You as others' voices carry too much weight in my life.

Reveal the people and false messages that draw me away from You, my first love. Help me trust You fully instead of leaning on my own understanding. Show me how to live in Your light so I stand firm in the faith.

Amen.

GLORY TO JESUS

"Father, the hour has come. Glorify
Your Son, that Your Son may glorify You."

JOHN 17:1

Lord,

Thank You, Lord, for Your Son, Jesus Christ. You saved me from my sin through His death on the cross. You brought me into Your family, filled me with Your Spirit, and secured my future so I can be with You forever. I'm no longer Your enemy because You call me Your friend!

Through glorifying Your Son, You brought glory to Yourself. As Your child, reveal Your glory in me as I surrender my life fully to You. Like Jesus, give me humility to serve and sacrifice. Strengthen me with His courage to suffer.

Fill me with Jesus' selfless love for You, Your people, and this lost world until the day You bring me home. May I give You glory in all I do and say.

Amen.

YOU ARE WORTHY

You are worthy, our Lord and God,
to receive glory and honor and power,
for You created all things,
and by Your will they were created
and have their being.

REVELATION 4:11

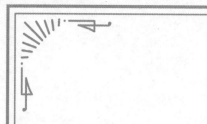

ABOUT THE AUTHORS

Rob Teigen is a bestselling author, podcast host, and the co-founder of Growing Home Together. Rob and his wife, Joanna, are the parents of five kids and are committed to creating resources to care for the soul of your family.

Josh Teigen is a husband and father who is passionate about sharing stories of God's work in people's lives through his ministry, Banner Media. Josh and his wife, Cassie, make their home in West Michigan and actively serve in their local church.

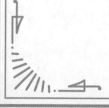